Hemisphere Eleven

HEMISPHERE ELEVEN

N

HWØRDE

gnOme books
gnomebooks.wordpress.com

Please address inquiries to:
gnomebooks@gmail.com

Cover image: José de Ribera, *Magdalena penitente*. Public domain:
https://commons.wikimedia.org/wiki/File:Ribera_-_Magdalena_penitente_-_Prado_-_1.jpg

Back cover image: José de Ribera, *Prometheus*. Public domain:
https://commons.wikimedia.org/wiki/File:Prometeo_(Jos%C3%A9_de_Ribera).jpg

ISBN-13: ISBN-13: 978-0692631478 (HWØRDE)
ISBN-10: 069263147X

A discontinuous continuation of fallen, unfollowable imperatives, numbering one thousand three hundred and sixty-one.

"When they came back from the tomb, they told all these things to the Eleven" (Luke 24:9).

1361 is the 218th prime number. 1 + 3 + 6 + 1 = 11 = 2 +1 + 8.

1. Talk in bubbles on the verge of spheres.
2. Perish with every breath in overwhelming astonishment.
3. Be so far gone that you never arrived.
4. Have no idea.
5. Be so clueless that every clue is itself eternally stunned by its own inexistence.
6. Obliterate multiverses by means of bewilderment.
7. Lose yourself so far in disbelief that everything is absolutely, unintelligibly true.
8. Wonder so horribly why anything is happening at all that it never did.
9. Mercilessly send all your questions back to the omnipresent front lines.
10. Fail to meet me for fear of being swallowed alive by an enormous question.
11. Fall into the gaping abyss under your feet until you shoot up out of the ground.
12. Writhe in unknowing.
13. Live in the midst of continual well-coordinated all-out attacks upon everything you ever felt or thought was true.
14. Be always already pierced inexplicably by yet another incommunicable arrow.
15. Watch the world vanish like mist before the glorious sun of secret maximal confusion.

16. Leave me behind so fast that you bump into me in infinite regress.
17. Give everyone a look that shows what they are in for.
18. Lay your life aside in favor of becoming a cosmically autophagous query.
19. See human knowledge for what it is: a messy mass of poorly formulated search terms.
20. Drink wine of bewilderment until the tears wash away your face.
21. Erase every trace of yourself with a free lifetime supply of the Ointment of Mystification.
22. Think about something by evaporating the thought.
23. Act in way that effectively accuses all entities of insufficient astonishment.
24. Follow yourself off the cliff of supreme bafflement.
25. Leap like a child for joy into the arms of spontaneous senseless distress.
26. Indulge profoundly in the pleasure of forgetting everything people say.
27. Offer everything as a reward to anyone who successfully steals all your answers.
28. Infinitely reverse the ontological order of answer and question.
29. Immediately become incapable of following any directions other than the irrepressible hunch that you are absolutely and hopelessly lost.

30. Dive into delightful epistemological hopelessness past the point of actually needing to do away with yourself.
31. Abandon inner connection to all persons who think they know what they are talking about.
32. Exploit your friends to bust all of you out of the prison of knowledge.
33. Deliberately refuse to know, no matter what the world offers you.
34. Develop courage for greater and greater bewilderment by remembering all who have died in the depths of ignorance.
35. Wonder why one ever bothered to.
36. Fail to believe how you ever fell for it.
37. Make no difference between small and great matters that do not make sense.
38. Know not what to do, think, feel, or say.
39. Place no secret hope in your fatal astonishment.
40. Figure out a way off the island of being that does not involve figuring anything out.
41. Suspect everything.
42. Renounce your bewilderment for nothing except greater and greater bewilderment.
43. Know so little that the whole universe flocks to you for meaningless questions.
44. Let no light ever escape the black hole of your non-knowledge.
45. Offer no explanation, give nothing away.
46. Die of unknowing.

47. Remain unintelligible, especially to omniscience.
48. Thrive by robbing yourself in the apophatic alleys of radically immanent auto-blindness.
49. Eclipse all knowing in the perfect pitch blackness of your pupil.
50. Wonder why until why itself never made any sense in the first place or ever will.
51. Expose your whole system to the plague of inexplicability.
52. Hypothetically blame everything on everything in order to be even more astonished by all that remains unaccounted for.
53. Crack open your skull like lightning on the stone of total astonishment.
54. Bask in the glory of bewilderment.
55. Enjoy only the intolerable.
56. Drift al di là in gravitationAL DIstraction.
57. See that every line is the horizon.
58. Expand by inhaling the universe through your navel.
59. Observe yourself looking up at the stars like a blind and dumb beast.
60. Alternate seamlessly between hypersensitive dullness and adamantine interoception.
61. Become numb enough to feel everything everywhere.
62. Come down with a hopeless case of yourself.

63. Shamelessly endure the shame.
64. Battle all demons everywhere all at once all the time.
65. Infinitely resign to being more and more lost.
66. Follow the wind forever the moment before it arrives.
67. Demand nothing from the future.
68. Think like a pebble in a glass of water.
69. Die one birth at a time.
70. Be no longer able to think what you will never stop thinking about.
71. Drop it into the well beneath your feet without making a wish.
72. Know why and say nothing.
73. Replace your head with the moon.
74. Sense the occult inclination of one's skeleton.
75. Only take NO for an answer.
76. Lose face entirely facing the fact that nothing will suffice.
77. No longer know what you want.
78. Nullify.
79. Don't fall for another intellectual thinking intelligently about (the) nothing.
80. Wonder what will never become of us.
81. Confuse fear of flying with desire to fall.
82. Confound need to climb with capacity to sink.
83. Substitute walking for sleeping and vice versa.

84. Replace taking-steps with going-to-the-end-and-coming-out-the-other-side.
85. Look at the world and think, 'and I wanted to add to *that*?'
86. Somehow overcome the monster you become by fighting it.
87. Stare down the abyss not big enough for the both of us.
88. Think what you would be like without the world in it.
89. Throw me back like a fish into what has no foundation.
90. Perish fast enough.
91. Blithely go about your business in secret trembling.
92. Bang your head on the stone of astonishment until you either go mad or become something else.
93. Operate by means of mere presence.
94. Fail to know whether you are dying or waking up.
95. Entirely forget to call for help.
96. Do it by having no idea what to do.
97. Make it harder by thinking that it could not be any harder.
98. Discover one day what it is like to be as miserable as you actually are.
99. Be trapped in a nightmare of your own unmaking.
100. Listen to the call, obey the imperative, unend the infinitive.
101. Hear it all boil down to the ability to remain silent and walk away.

N

102.	Conspire with everything.
103.	Feverishly pace the universe in melodramatic paleness.
104.	Birth the conjoined miracle of death-in-life and life-in-death.
105.	Listen to the music that prevails over words when we speak.
106.	Find you where I uncover me.
107.	Take careless care of the amorphous matter running through you.
108.	Dissipate the unshaped germ of soul into a breath's mystical air.
109.	Hunt every blossom-seed upon the heart's hyper-wild wind.
110.	Peel me away from myself and take everything away.
111.	Draw yourself into the noose of uncircumscribable honesty.
112.	Drink sweetest dreams in the tomb-kiss of eternal moonlight.
113.	Drink soul-storm waves of everything-nothing from the dark sea flooding through me.
114.	Die to slurp-drink the infinite wine-drop surplus.
115.	Inexhale the outinward breath-spring wafting me back out into your nothing-being.
116.	Constantly stir the cauldron-turbulence to maintain perfect burning.
117.	Drag me down to the very top.
118.	Spend another day dying as usual.

119. Fight continually the fantastic conceit that you know what you are doing here.
120. Help (me).
121. Unanchor your ship from the clouds.
122. Sail through the closed open twin doors of the horizon.
123. Crawl happily off to die battling desire all day long because everything is your fault and you are not you.
124. Respire in air pockets among rocks deep in the heart-sea.
125. Fool yourself with honesty.
126. Find a way to the wayless.
127. Go inwardly a million miles farther than you ever have.
128. Stop asking the wrong question.
129. See the contradiction in you.
130. Plunge into pure difference from everything.
131. Contribute to nothing.
132. Plead to no one.
133. Stop hugging yourself.
134. Have nowhere to go, ever.
135. Keep your eyes peeled for/by the horizon.
136. Return the world through a word into liquid crystal fire.
137. Regard yourself to be no more than a dung worm.
138. Add nothing to nothing for the sake of everything.
139. Inhibit your face from helping everyone make the wrong decision.

140. Come to the end of yourself in seconds flat—no time at all.
141. Don't miss the opportunity to no longer have time for yourself.
142. Get out of my way by making me trip over myself.
143. Nix the next.
144. Solve the world.
145. Observe yourself committing a crime outrageously perpetrated and perpetually unsolved by means of its own overwhelming evidence.
146. Halve the time of your unlife.
147. Be torn open by oneness.
148. Know that no one knows it and just isn't saying.
149. Let it hit you over and over again.
150. Cherish the fact of being more lost now than ever.
151. Know that no one knows and that no one wants to.
152. Lick the cleanness of the sword that cuts everything in half.
153. Effortlessly annihilate all things in the infinite heat of the criterion of absolute certainty.
154. Walk at the speed at which time stops.
155. Live on the other side of language.
156. Be omnipotently unable.
157. Pluck the diadem from your own skull and cast it into the sea.
158. Perish indifferently.
159. Wonder never again about nothing.

160. Wander happily among the never-were.
161. Know what it means to not.
162. Contemplate that which meaning never means.
163. Leap into the hole from which everything has already returned.
164. Have no idea ever what is happening to you.
165. Fearlessly live the secret, unutterable life that no one possesses.
166. Step through me at the moment I step through you.
167. Sink upward inside an immeasurable weight of feeling far beyond the human scale.
168. Never again confuse the there with the real.
169. Let every fact experience itself.
170. Crank up the scream of unknowing until no one can hear themselves think.
171. Follow everything beyond everything.
172. Renounce everything not running away but through it, by running it through everything with the point of renunciation.
173. Make black one with black . . . make love/gold.
174. Mate love with itself.
175. Capture the Mother in the net of your own puppet strings and no more be a machine.
176. Use your beak energy not to blab but to poke through the eggshell.

177. Tear open into oneness.
178. Cook everything in the salt of your tears.
179. See that I am naked overneath my body.
180. Ride the chariot of cyclones straight into the jungle.
181. Seek self-replacement, not self-improvement.
182. Abandon the urge to bother other people.
183. Stop paying attention to anything at all.
184. Stop hiding out in yourself, you little weirdo.
185. Meet in the mo( )rning where we are not.
186. Blame no one for anything, blame everyone for everything.
187. Recapture the jaguar of your mind in the jungle of completeness.
188. Pave a way from within.
189. Observe maximum astonishment at minimum distance.
190. Eat yourself through the face hole of all-consuming homesickness.
191. Be my deadline.
192. Peel back sky and face in one movement.
193. Keep your eye on the autodeadline between everything and itself.
194. Weep yourself under the rug.
195. Be squeezed through your skin by the weight of everything.
196. Be sent into a spin by the sheer fun.
197. Grow hungrier for nothing.

198. Make a clear choice between: a) ignorance; b) hypocrisy; c) absolute mental annihilation.
199. Know the pain of being trapped like a reflection in a teardrop.
200. Stand still hitting the wall of yourself at faster than light speed.
201. Wake once again into the vastness of the uni-worse.
202. Overdo and overthink everything in hopeless pursuit of perpetual overastonishment.
203. Stay at home and doom doom all day long until you die.
204. Be filled with the Whole by feeding on Nothing.
205. Bask in the absence of priority between form and formlessness.
206. Find a playmate with infinite attributes who has none.
207. Discriminate between dreaming and not-dreaming by seeing whether there is a world out there or not.
208. Remain in a state of final evaporation.
209. Outgrow the incurable disease of oneself.
210. Let my body rise from me.
211. Resurrect your body before death.
212. Die before it is too late.
213. See in the mirror that the reality of your problem is the unreality of you.
214. Do everything all at once forever.
215. Only make plans as if you do not exist.

216. Drift on the pure plane of planlessness.
217. Seek only the peace of peak-desperation.
218. Write yourselves away, auto-fishing backwards with hook-words spewed by a double-mouth.
219. Go swimming where the water is the shark and the shark is the water.
220. Get it bad.
221. Embrace the disappearing skin of distance.
222. Speak my ear.
223. Understand that this darkness is itself the highest elevation of your mind.
224. Apply as normal then return to idiot-savant status once accepted.
225. Flow like an infinite blob.
226. Abort thyself.
227. Hang me by the heels until your pail is filled with my tears.
228. Epiphanize the obvious.
229. Sail the seven seas in a scholarship of fools.
230. Fall into the absence of fall-back positions.
231. Cut through the cloak of complacency calling itself contentment.
232. Feel like (a) sap from a very very old tree.
233. Realize hand-holding as the idea of ideas.
234. Speak in preemptive quotations, avant le texte.

235. Begin with a simple yes, writing a humid could with the body.
236. Enjoy the flavor of the fluidity of the half-born in its authentic state.
237. Planlessly unroll the floor-horizon into a sky-ceiling.
238. Know that whatever you think you are accomplishing with your life, you are not.
239. Cut the fastest cut, the one that cuts nothing without a knife.
240. Drink forever from the so-intoxicating abyss of inexistent wine.
241. Bow uneasily to the almighty X.
242. Indulge the sheer pleasure of doing what you have to refrain from.
243. Fly through walking through your fear.
244. Fail to cope with the insurmountable sorrow of existing.
245. Want to break out of wanting through an outbreak of total breakout.
246. Implode by exhaling individuation.
247. Drive your drives, take them for a ride.
248. Nail your eyes to X.
249. Bring me the head of the horizon.
250. Burn the horizon for spheresy.
251. See in the light of submarine caverns.
252. Run from the horizon until it chases you.
253. Solve your brain into a puzzle that comes together only as a blind image of itself.

254. Splash through puddles of positive self-forgetfulness.
255. Gag me with a thinking button.
256. Walk in circles with chronos looking for aion.
257. Turn your worry inside out.
258. Think another's thought without having to think it.
259. Be only the agent of what needs infinite preparation—be worthlessly worthwhile.
260. Be THAT you are.
261. Approach everything as huge trick making you lose by thinking you can win.
262. Be careful, lest near madness get too close to itself.
263. Start with the finished sculpture and hollow it out from the inside.
264. Do not wait for me to be disappointed.
265. Dive into the zerOcean.
266. Comprehend the double illusion of knowledge and ignorance.
267. Bathe like a child in the mirror of the black horizon.
268. Follow the sigh to ghazal street, where the gazelles sigh.
269. Emancipate the horizon by caging it into chasing you.
270. End me to mend.
271. Die on pilgrimage to the origin of that one sigh.

272. Distill all words, feelings, thoughts, and dreams down into one impossibly sweet teardrop.
273. Return to silence in the present light of absence, the absent light of presence.
274. Take the abyss-elevator to here.
275. Succumb to saying nothing in full body stutter.
276. Think yourself to sleep in a horizon-deprivation tank.
277. Let it get too serious.
278. Build a skyscraper to escape the sky.
279. Interrupt the interruption into an accelerated eruption.
280. Commune autophagously after an alpine plane crash.
281. Survive by imagining the worst.
282. Self-liquify inside the threshold of sorrow-petrification and full-body stutter.
283. Allow time to mourn eternity.
284. Hesitantly accept the mortal happiness of horrorloveoplean humiliation.
285. Become a clean mess.
286. Take yourself out with the garbage.
287. Tight rope walk on the tension of your own bow.
288. Find the way out of a loop in the loop itself.
289. Surf a moebius soliton wave into its missing side.
290. Become an angel to the Outside.
291. Be jolted by the Bolt of Joy.

292.   Plant your throat-lump in Paradise.
293.   Find no search results for "the universe is a tomb."
294.   Involute into a four-dimensional ectomorph.
295.   Wear tesseract jeans.
296.   Die by looking forward to seeing NOW— eternally—this moment of looking forward to seeing it.
297.   Successfully pronounce the sevenfold tongue-twister of sexlessness.
298.   Take the detour to the detour.
299.   Come with instructions how to operate yourself.
300.   Consume my future.
301.   Please take it away.
302.   Embody the event-cube.
303.   Profit from selling your junkself to no one for free.
304.   No longer wander between many possible objects of similar experience.
305.   See, namely, that the hole in your heart is the universe.
306.   Be this body, the one that cannot be— decapitated.
307.   Shine brightly in the sun, like a dead dog's white teeth.
308.   Discard relative values in favor of the intrinsic worth of everything.
309.   Live constantly in a state of fortifying collapse.
310.   Sell everything into the mouth of infinity.

311. Buy me out of self-slavery.
312. Sell your freedom to the highest bidding cell.
313. Disown your self, own your corpse.
314. Shed your soul.
315. Slough off your inside.
316. Eviscerate your exterior.
317. Respond to what I haven't said.
318. Make notes in the invisible margin.
319. Discretely continue the infinite conversation.
320. Fiddle with time.
321. Play the flute of space.
322. Step into your lack of future.
323. Reinvent the past of never having been.
324. Be alone with everything.
325. Let your heart circumscribe the lonely universe.
326. Adopt the garb of an unknown kind of entity.
327. Talk to me in abundant ellipses.
328. See that what you don't see is keeping you company.
329. Populate black.
330. Look at the horizon as into the bottomless wound of the universe.
331. Heal the universe-wound from the inside.
332. Nurse everything into extinction.
333. Let the abyss plunge in on you.
334. Observe the aura of your solar plexus in the eclipse of my pupil.
335. Say the stupidity of thought.

336. Proceed no further than the cusp of yourself.
337. Stop right here pretending to know where you are.
338. Circumambulate the universal mountain by neither moving nor being moved in spiral spheres.
339. Wind space-time into a ball around the pole of your most perfect swerve.
340. Do the nothing there is to do.
341. Soul-rise straight from the bed of dreams like a shaft of golden wheat ready for reaping.
342. Become the punchline of a joke no one will ever understand.
343. Think everything is normal again only to find out that it is even more upside down in a worse better way.
344. See all things from the other side of the abyss.
345. Know that there is no this.
346. Suffer from strange outbursts of joy that rob you of the strength to express or even feel them.
347. Stay open, staring in blank astonishment that.
348. Swim the horizon far beyond the sea of feeling.
349. Drop the umbrella of time.
350. Scream the (spiritual) scream.
351. Hack through the hallucination of relevance.
352. Notice that everything works perfectly.

353. Disburden me of the fake idea-feeling that I am my body.
354. Figure out nothing.
355. Bite and be bitten by your own steps.
356. Be the one one cannot think without thinking of.
357. Scream as many silent screams as it takes to get to the omnipresent center of everything.
358. Grow al di là.
359. Fly your book-moth into the flame of love-heresy.
360. Inhale your heart-smoke like an inquisitor.
361. Burn your own heart for heresy.
362. Drink from the empty chalice that overflows the moment it touches your lips.
363. Draw wine from a bottle that fills you without being opened.
364. Start feeling at home in a bottomless shaft.
365. Give in to the giant gravity lifting you off the ground.
366. Know nothing other than that you are not here.
367. Get over yourself.
368. See dissolution's both ends.
369. Be fool.
370. Learn the stupidity which does not call itself stupid.
371. Throw back the javelin of thrownness, re-gift the gift of givenness.

372. See eye to eye with that which perforates you from the inside, peeping out through all the holes.
373. Veer towards veering, come close to closeness, depart departure.
374. Try to find a replacement for air.
375. Program the programmer to fail.
376. Bump into the dark.
377. Persist in a kind of volatile transparency.
378. Spook thought into looking.
379. Climb as mountain falling upward.
380. Trip the trap of thought so that it stops you in your tracks.
381. Take aim at the convergence of all arrows in the absence of any claim.
382. Rebuild the wall blown down by the storm with a beautiful window.
383. Ground thyself in shock—shock thyself in ground.
384. Float in the tomb of a spiral abyss.
385. Orient thyself everywhere towards something with no place to go.
386. Steal the fire by mimicking the gods.
387. Be no match for the one who holds you upside down.
388. Enjoy the secret extent to which madness of love is love of madness.
389. Look at what people say, listen to the look on their faces.
390. Heed nothing that tells you what you want.
391. Get drunk feeling sorry that you have no self to feel sorry for.

392. Fall just enough and in the right direction, then step upward on falling.
393. Stare at that which is eclipsed behind everything.
394. Know that, were things any more absurd, they would exist.
395. Celebrate the bad news: it has nothing to do with you.
396. As soon as it happens, think again.
397. Give in and plunge now into the plunge to be taken anyway.
398. Hear the tear that trickles into your ear whisper itself.
399. Be devoured by a four dimensional panther with stars for teeth.
400. Die, and never stop dying, until you are no longer dead.
401. Sculpt oneself at the threshold where sound and body are one substance.
402. Stretch your mouth into a megaphone to receive a scream from the other side.
403. Pierce through the hyper-illusion of coming to your senses.
404. Fold your phantasms into origami.
405. Play hide and seek with nowhere to hide and nothing to seek.
406. Swim from the shore of dreaming into the middle of the very first stone.
407. Leap faster than light into the sermon of your petrified self.
408. Take a stroll hanging by the hook of THAT.

409. Centrifugally hide seeking the center everywhere and nowhere.

410. Touch the point upon which wanting anything at all becomes absolutely painful.

411. Peep through the bullet ( )hole with a pupil whose gaze eXplicates the assassination of the fourfold.

412. Steer by way of night the titanic of thought into the iceberg.

413. Hang out with what is hyperchaotically off the hook.

414. Translate every name as *boo!*

415. Distinguish no longer between form and formlessness.

416. Gaze upon things like two mirrors looking at each other and seeing nothing but everything all the way down.

417. Remain distracted by the not yet.

418. Have it by wanting without wanting to have what you want.

419. Foreshorten your attention span by the height of the Beloved's stature.

420. Be infinitely more doomed than you will ever know.

421. Use your body to disidentify with it, identify with your body to disuse it.

422. Say everything as commentary on the nothing one has to say.

423. Observe the absolute impossibilization of the about.

424. Lonesomely hear the screech of the owl who alone hears your lament.

425. Tell your body to abandon the idea that there is an abyss to hold it.
426. Intensify the abyssic twinness of the impossible and the actual.
427. Discover that the text was all along only a commentary on its margin.
428. Constantly succeed at failing to not feel hopeless.
429. Feel continually on the verge of flying wherever whenever you want.
430. Leap suddenly over everything all at once.
431. Minimize absolutely the aim to please a maximum of others.
432. See that a lost happiness was no happiness at all.
433. Subtract the total percentage of talk and discussion secretly aimed towards avoidance of direct understanding.
434. Encourage the world to do the nothing it can do for or against you.
435. Demolish the false foundation of all fear.
436. Pay closest attention to what does not concern you.
437. See the true horror by watching your face.
438. Defriend that which says the world is yours to change.
439. Listen to criticism's primary communication: the habit of criticism.
440. Live the miraculous transition from never existing to no longer existing.

441. Pay no attention to the rumors you are spreading about yourself.
442. Swim in the air of stupefaction.
443. Cross eyes to the point that vision sees itself.
444. Accomplish what you cannot by seeing that you cannot.
445. Let life come and go into your life as it wishes.
446. Admit to infinite embarrassment over being what you are.
447. See what no one wants to: that the whole show is itself only spectatorship, that the speculation is only a spectacle.
448. Never again collaborate with yourself.
449. Leave behind the way of being which is overtaken by being in the way.
450. Stare at what all day watches itself, never seeing where it actually is, wanting incessantly to not know.
451. Watch carefully who talks about who.
452. Be eternal now, like the sound of light on snow.
453. Spin in the dizziness that gravity feels.
454. Discern the desire behind every syllogism, s(p)lice the will across the decision of its own cut.
455. Tunnel through the tunnel you are inside, inside the tunnel you are.
456. Rise by no longer thinking you are awake.
457. Evade not the problem by looking for solutions.

458. Hear the sound of the entity who laughs out loud every time it makes sense when you think something but not when you say it.

459. Accept that which is always making sure you will never be cured of seeing something as divine.

460. Curse the thought that thinks it is in the world.

461. Perceive clearly that all systems are creations of confusion.

462. Stick with what has no opposite.

463. Never listen to the pitch.

464. Knock off everything you are doing because you are afraid to stop doing it.

465. Be eaten alive by the words coming out of your mouth.

466. Learn to handle the fact that the whole universe is created to keep everything from you because you cannot handle anything.

467. Fall through the floor of your tomb to find yourself suddenly floating through a higher sub-horizon.

468. Learn every moment how to live with an invisible lance in your side.

469. Know that it is not a good idea to hang onto ideas.

470. Defeat thyself into victory.

471. Watch yourself thinking thoughts which lead nowhere until an explosion occurs.

472. Stop making everything worse by talking about yourself.

473. No longer be impressed by impressive things.
474. Try to have fun swimming in the outer reaches of Reality's distance from itself.
475. Taste the part of you hungry enough to consume the horizon, tired enough to swallow time.
476. Be filled by what crushes you.
477. Hear the tone of silence that stops eternity.
478. Rurn the world through a word into liquid crystal fire.
479. Swallow a teaspoon of sighs every morning to help unravel your throat lump into a spiral sphere.
480. Set warp drive to the black hole formed from the supernova of your stardom in a 13.8-billion-year-long mental movie.
481. Look forward to what has already destroyed you.
482. Never say anything ever again.
483. Perish inside a silent love-scream from beyond al di là.
484. Exchange the parachute of hypothesis for wings of bewilderment.
485. Hold hands with your head and lead it who knows where.
486. Escape in the bubble-trap of a higher-sinking underwater sigh.
487. Speak near to something so naturally mad and madly natural.
488. Die trapped inside a beauty you cannot see.

489. Fall awake listening to a strange new scent that lights the entire world.
490. Reach beyond everything by grabbing a hold that can only be grasped by thrusting your arm through a hole in yourself.
491. Be totally shot through and through with a secret need.
492. Speak only in mutually recursive auto-citation.
493. Find the energy to finally fall asleep.
494. Fall through the ground from an excess of wings.
495. Feed hell's mouth to itself through a three-headed dog which has more heads than it needs.
496. Never stop perceiving the actual steepness of all things.
497. Find the point as fast as possible where crucifixion is the loveliest relief.
498. Allow yourself to be as astonished as you want to be.
499. To watch your head spin off at the mere thought of a name.
500. Quickly become the sound of the mallet as it strikes the stake being driven into your heart.
501. To be one who loses his mind, never seeing anything ever again, except in your dreams.
502. Sink to the seafloor under the weight of inescaping sighs.

N

503. Lack the strength to fail, find the
weakness to win.
504. Don't know how to do it.
505. Afflict the remedy.
506. Learn nothing over and over again.
507. Have a life no longer.
508. Evaporate through a wrinkle in time.
509. Sit back, relax, and let your mind snap.
510. Unveil ever new sublevels of self-
limitation.
511. Disentangle nothing from nothing.
512. Collapse fatally under the weight of
everything, then suddenly get up and go
for a jog like nothing ever happen.
513. Specialize in all kinds of nothing.
514. Look forward to where you are.
515. Stare all night long into the sunset of the
universe.
516. Want everything and do nothing about
it—do everything and want nothing of it.
517. Stand still in the flame between your
eyes.
518. Say the same nothing over and over
again—always new.
519. Dive all at once into the one direction.
520. Feel how it feels to have all your wishes
hopelessly fulfilled—the wish for
hopelessness.
521. Stop telling yourself anything.
522. Run out of yourself.
523. Cherishly cherish the moments and
hours when everything melts and all is

revealed without anyone being there to see it.

524. Trust no one, starting with you.

525. Wish that one could say, being almost infinitely more happy that one cannot.

526. Taste the silent bite of the soul as it bores like a drill through the deepest ocean floor.

527. Quickly uncorrupt thyself.

528. Drown the spheres, unleash the tide of sighs.

529. Consecrate thyself to Silence.

530. Involute the original Want.

531. Fail to arrive by being already there.

532. Accept what you have become: a buffoon, a monster, a one-sided abyss.

533. Find happiness: the fact that nothing can make you happy.

534. See the world for what it is: further proof that you are not being honest with yourself.

535. Spend no more than a week with yourself.

536. Being left behind by everything, leave everything behind being.

537. Have enough of words.

538. Polish all day the spear point of perfect abandonment.

539. To thine own nausea be true.

540. Point yourself to the exit.

541. Change your name to "Exit."

542. Observe yourself seeing that you are not anything you see.

543. Stop trying to con truth.
544. Unveil the multiverse where talking is possible.
545. Accelerate to the speed at which nothing ever happens.
546. Don't.
547. Stop life from thinking life away by thinking it has a life.
548. Sterilize the infectee of feeling thwarted.
549. Become so clear you can't see it.
550. Take it ALL.
551. Want nothing from nobody.
552. Think and see like sand in the oyster of omniscience.
553. Lose everyone.
554. Ask why they ask you your name.
555. Don't take your word for it.
556. Observe yourself as the blindspot of everything.
557. Continue what never began, end what never continues, begin what never will end.
558. Erase the faintest idea of where you really are.
559. Accuse everything of being itself.
560. Understand the failure of being understood.
561. Imagine how deeply asleep you are in order to be dreaming your life away in this universe.
562. Embrace the infinity of hyper-significant irrelevance.

563. Embrace three times the moment of seeing that you own body is a ghost.
564. Exist for the first time again.
565. Be eternally what will never have been.
566. Let what whatever happens to have never happened.
567. Actually no longer be.
568. Pinpoint the site where one's irides, bleeding razor tears, cut a pupil on the horizon.
569. Feel so everything.
570. Be afraid of how afraid you really are.
571. Reduce to tautology excitement and despair.
572. Remind the question not to forget who is asking it.
573. Leap into lifting the impossible veil—yourself.
574. Know every moment that you have wasted your entire life.
575. Diagram the point at which overness is over.
576. Cherish the degree of honesty that no one wants.
577. Die fighting the eternal war between THIS and THAT.
578. Pre-escape the trap of expectation.
579. Smile for the first time.
580. Say no to the person who is masquerading as you.
581. Play back the recording of all your nervous laughter for our listening pleasure.

582. Undrink the drop of every desire into the ocean of . . .
583. See without you being there.
584. Accidentally lose your head on purpose.
585. Earn a degree of separation between art and laziness.
586. Burst at the SEEMS.
587. Spot immediately how mixed up I really am.
588. Reform the one who is trying to change conditions.
589. Lose nothing by taking away everything that never was in the first place.
590. Lean everything against everything until all falls down.
591. Beware any language you want to hear.
592. Discover whether there is an alternative to the nothingness you call something.
593. Explain why your vast knowledge means nothing.
594. Fail everyone and everything.
595. Rise like a sun vanishing from the face of life.
596. Wake up less than lost in the invisible dark.
597. Find a way to exist without existing.
598. Have nothing to offer no one.
599. Consider the maximum seriousness with which anything has ever been considered.
600. Live an infinity of lives that never happen.
601. Ask why you are human.

602. Live now in negative time.
603. Amass evidence of everything not being there.
604. Take the path of no return.
605. Apologize on behalf of the universe.
606. Crush yourself to death with a simple realization that no one understands.
607. Perform the stage with no one on it.
608. Be the dream that, beyond this world, produces worldly dreams.
609. Be the world that, beyond this dream, produces dreamy worlds.
610. Succumb to the incurable ecstasy of the incurable.
611. Blindly obey the law of the conservation of consciousness.
612. See that the mirror is insane.
613. Consider the smell of scorched wings as the moth's perfume.
614. Seize the impossibility of conscious complaint.
615. Not to do without doing, but to not do without not doing.
616. Eat the cockroach as it crawls across the page of thought.
617. Face the fact that you have absolutely no idea how to live.
618. Avoid the pandemic of phony casualness.
619. Live in totally different worlds.
620. Amass overwhelming evidence that the universe is not even the tip of the iceberg.

621. Draw that which everything is a diagram of.

622. Speak to the one before whom all words say nothing.

623. Seek only that which has already taken everything away.

624. Bury at least one of the many sources of all life's problems: the idea that you are alive.

625. Know too well who the abandonment of who will never abandon you is.

626. Never know what to think.

627. Leave yourself alone.

628. Want everything to have nothing, want nothing to have everything.

629. Actually be what never exists, to actually do what never happens.

630. Summarize the whole situation in seven incomplete sentences.

631. Appall thyself ever more with the spiral storm in your heart.

632. Have no choice but to actually become the reality one is.

633. Be nearly certain from afar that a second close encounter will be fatal.

634. Secretly do for the sake of . . . what no one will ever understand.

635. Wake now, one by one, in the place where all are sleeping.

636. Be crucified on the horizon.

637. Stop saying and start doing all that you ever said.

638. Take all the garbage out in one piece, the only piece of garbage.
639. Make it atop the spiral, with or without yourself.
640. Sew your wounds up with the one true lie.
641. Feel the time that time feels.
642. Embrace the misfortune of being that which makes one want nothing.
643. Walk on the inside of the horizon.
644. Forever remain friends with the unsurvivable.
645. Care only about one thing without having any clue what it is.
646. Renounce the life-dream as not yours.
647. Unmask the dramatics of being in trouble.
648. See that it is not happening—this is.
649. Stand imperially alone in the presence of sky.
650. Trace freedom to the void.
651. Stay in the game by remaining outside.
652. Be something that eternal omniscience somehow failed to notice and will never mention.
653. Do not die not knowing how shallow you really are.
654. Drown before it's too late.
655. Be unsure whether you did not wake up or did not fall asleep.
656. Hang out with what is left when the world leaves the world.

657.   Unconvince yourself that you are a
         concerned citizen.
658.   Remain at a total loss minus remaining
         at a total loss.
659.   Fill nature's horror of emptiness with
         spirit's horror of fullness.
660.   Be gone, still here, past having been,
         again before being.
661.   Consciously wake up.
662.   Unknow everything about the ocean
         except how to swim.
663.   Communicate with yourself on a need-
         to-know basis.
664.   Take the first step toward destroying an
         illusion: seeing that you are it.
665.   No longer go.
666.   Only read books that read your
         thoughts.
667.   Sever the head that refuses to feel what
         the heart knows.
668.   Cut out the heart that refuses to know
         what the head feels.
669.   Hold back the sea with a smile.
670.   Get out and see the world: presence of
         the absence of self-negation.
671.   Agree that the dream is beyond this
         world.
672.   Find the treasure found simply by not
         seeking anything else.
673.   Follow directions nowhere.
674.   Break the bars of this prison that never
         existed.

675. Transcribe in silent breath the word your blood speaks.
676. Give up altogether on there being a way to be.
677. Prove once and for all, by doing absolutely nothing, that there is absolutely nothing to fear.
678. Feed the world thoughts that make it ashamed of thinking.
679. Conjure an entity who abandons language the moment it appears.
680. Fast forward the seed into a bomb.
681. Slow down the catastrophe to a day at the beach.
682. Endure the preference for abstraction as a sign of incipient love.
683. Accept infinitely in advance the prospect of an absolute disproportion.
684. Wonder whatever happened to yourself.
685. Stop everything, except the beginning of the end and the end of the beginning.
686. Cloak the mystery in nothing but its own light.
687. Meet yourself by sending an invitation to no one.
688. Surpass me by going slower.
689. Fall behind by going faster.
690. Earn an A+ for flunking.
691. Choose whether there are: a) no rules and none follow them; b) only rules and all follow them; c) no rules and all follow them; d) only rules and none follow

them; e) all of the above; f) none of the above.

692. Forget that which remembers everything.
693. Remember that which forgets everything.
694. See yourself as nothing but an unwillingness to see yourself.
695. Be totally clueless for no reason what to do or say about anything.
696. Be too busy for the time being to be in time.
697. Find out whatever became of that student who misread all philosophy as an instruction to do something.
698. Ponder neither the ponderables nor the imponderables.
699. Attend a mass demonstration in which everyone rises in protest against themselves.
700. Sit not in a cave, thinking cold thought, leaving to others to do as you ought.
701. Embrace and evade the curse at the same time.
702. Delete your default position before the end of this sentence.
703. Share the obvious secret absolute non-difference between loving everything and caring about nothing.
704. Seek pardon for having been.
705. Take the blame for your own birth.
706. Listen to your heart beat aloud in the endless dark.

707. Have everything to show for yourself.
708. Stop acting like.
709. Sense your body as the smoke of a soul burning slowly in hell.
710. Know that death is coming and you are it.
711. Be born tattooed with yourself.
712. Go where there is nowhere to go.
713. Refuse to know without knowing how to know.
714. Mark the point where space refuses to exist.
715. Feel free to stand nearer at night to your dream window.
716. Kiss light.
717. Forget whose turn it is to take the runaway train of melo-terror for a spin.
718. Fit through, not in.
719. Clearly see that you have every reason to fear nothing.
720. Have nothing to show for your self.
721. End my beginning. Begin my ending.
722. Unbegin my ending. Unend my beginning.
723. Simply accept that so much happens everywhere all the time that nothing ever happens anywhere at all.
724. Take no pills for the gnowsea, that mysterious periodic vertigo, like waves of nourishing hunger, induced by living in the present.
725. Don't care what the world is like.
726. Lose everything, starting with losing.

727. Smile with tears, laugh with sighs, moan with smiles, sob with cries.
728. Totally unravel.
729. Find happiness in the fact that nothing makes you happy.
730. Die by looking forward to waking from this dream.
731. Dream by looking forward to dying from this waking.
732. Wake by looking forward to dreaming this dying.
733. Die by looking forward to dreaming this waking.
734. Wake by looking forward to dying from this dreaming.
735. Dream by looking forward to waking from this death.
736. Feed your throat-lump to the sparrows and/or the cats.
737. Don't have enemies, let them have you.
738. Attend an event where fines and admission fees converge into a pure ticket, the price of doing nothing.
739. Seize the difficulty of deciding between absent presence and present absence.
740. Don't happen to be human.
741. See that I, the dreamer, is the dream of dreams.
742. Pursue philosophy as fear of being.
743. Let the spirit expand as life continues, crushing the heart with every breath.
744. Be so happy about the promise to meet that we have already met.

745. Take what you like because all things have already been taken away.
746. Give up what is keeping you from giving up, then give up giving up, then give up.
747. Close the gap between *I give up* and *give up I*.
748. Consider the almost intolerable excess of experience in every direction.
749. Never think that you can think.
750. See another kind of tear that shoots straight out of my pupil.
751. Fall into a well at the bottom of the sea.
752. Eliminate all problems by not being someone trying to fix a problem.
753. Taste the reason human beings think of God when they kill bugs.
754. Whatever you do, don't talk about the art.
755. Cancel your subscription to yourself—it expired at birth.
756. Please do not complicate the method by not applying it.
757. Stop making interesting points by speaking as if life were possible.
758. Make an indifference.
759. Lose the kind of hopelessness that thinks you will get something out of it.
760. Foster nothing.
761. Draw imaginary divisions because all divisions are imaginary.
762. Invite everything to attend nothing.
763. See that which guarantees delivery of all tears to their destination.

764. Unfulfill all your dreams one way or another.
765. Surf the point at which the tsunami finds itself proceeding without the hot air balloon.
766. Leave yourself behind to find me. Leave me behind to find no one. Leave no one behind to find you.
767. Meet the one who saw all you thought-felt-did when you were alone and was totally bored.
768. Suffer the pain of hearing the sound of silence as nothing saying everything to nothing.
769. Ask whether this hallucination is real or just a world.
770. Hear how every utterance as a failed attempt to understand what the words mean.
771. Fail at failing, flailing and flaying failure into a flying foil of the fall of falls.
772. Succumb to being perpetually struck down by the lightning virus
773. Leap nowhere by perishing in every direction.
774. Make a choice: either know what you are talking about or stop talking the way you do.
775. Be no less lost than I.
776. Combat the boredom of art with the art of boredom.
777. Photograph all the reflections in your tears.

778. Keep your attention everywhere all the time.
779. Avoid completely the problem with people being attracted by what other people do to attract them.
780. Do not try to steer the hot air balloon.
781. Unsolve the problem with expression.
782. See an opening of the eye of space, a sunrise the likes of which no one has seen.
783. Catch the overflow of void, surplus of zero, orgasm of nothing.
784. Let's run off together and leave ourselves alone.
785. Get ready: reality will be coming home any minute now.
786. Smell the grass and flowers growing over your grave.
787. Do as thou don't know what to do.
788. Let the world drown by hearing this thought.
789. Be where there is nothing to see.
790. Stop spotting what you want.
791. Gulp down the jolt to your entire system.
792. Sleepwalk the tightrope line between waking and dreaming.
793. Suddenly wake up in a million new ways at once.
794. Diagnose life with Cotardian delusion.
795. Follow the instruction to let everything fail.
796. Shatter the tragic pattern, split today.

797. Cherish the only thing it is impossible to detach oneself from.
798. Be deafened by unspeakable speech, drown in uncryable tears, die amid unsighable sighs.
799. Seize the opportunity of announcing the fact of your own death.
800. Be both wind and balloon.
801. Think about what head and body mean when they simultaneously say to each other 'get this thing off of me' with the same mouth.
802. Know nothing & feel nothing. Feel nothing & know everything. Know nothing & feel everything. Feel everything & know everything.
803. Let the page become a flash in which words realize that they are the one writing.
804. Know how good it is that your beauty is not yours, how true it is that you are not good.
805. Die as fresh as the day you were born.
806. Articulate the reason it seems like nothing ever happens.
807. Equate fear of death with desire to keep sleeping, for dreams do not want to wake up.
808. Take a stand against not seeing what is looking directly at you from all directions.
809. Stop not seeing the familiarity of everything.

810. Sit in the light, open your eyes, and enter the darkness.
811. Desire what you want more than wanting.
812. Think what will happen when you see that the sorrow in you is the same abyss as me.
813. Feel the overwhelming relief without ever finding it.
814. Put your finger on what you cannot consider.
815. Stay away from yourself faster than you can think.
816. Lose a life never yours.
817. Spread plague without becoming a pest.
818. Do not think that you are not pregnant.
819. See it everywhere without you, without you seeing it, without seeing that you are seeing it, without seeing, it.
820. Talk with the one whose silence is pure seduction.
821. Don't want to die because you do. Want to die because you don't.
822. Burn every moment the infinite letter expressing in perfect detail how you feel about everything.
823. Gaze upon the universe as an asymptotic search for real conversation.
824. Gather mounting evidence that you have not only fallen from, but were never on, your horse.

N

825. Never stop stumbling upon the invisible appearance of someone who makes doing anything impossible.
826. Burn with overwhelming desire to never say anything ever again.
827. Feel now that sinking feeling that this is not the afterlife yet.
828. Know that there is every reason to feel sorry for yourself because there is no self to feel sorry for.
829. Choose now between two options: a) to be someone and nothing; x) to be no one and everything.
830. Kiss the baby that cuts its own umbilical cord.
831. Lose all bearings save the invisible.
832. Love-hate the fear of the lack of aesthetics.
833. Be as embarrassed to be me as I am embarrassed to be you.
834. Amputate your third leg faster than it grows back.
835. Enjoy the conspiracy of itself.
836. Fail miserably at playing it cool.
837. Don't worry—everything is still over.
838. Speak on every topic with a touch of environy, the sense that place never quite resembles itself.
839. Hear what you hear, not want you want.
840. Stay here, or leave and come back when the pain becomes too great again.
841. Throw out the junk to find the jewel.

842. Remind yourself to forget. Forget yourself to remember. Recollect your mind. Dismember yourself.

843. Follow no one all the way home.

844. Let the footnotes speak for themselves.

845. Wish yourself good luck with THAT.

846. Be neither awake nor alive.

847. Meet the one you will only ever see again by never having been.

848. Shrink the distance between and the moment when you will have to forget everything that you ever learned.

849. Never again think that you haven't already lost.

850. Know that you are missing everything and be OK with it.

851. Meet me again in this world minus everything that never was.

852. Knock yourself out trying to think and know at the same time.

853. Die unknowing what you never missed.

854. Find something where you are not.

855. Take it anymore because you never have.

856. Hunt the jungle in the cage of the panther.

857. Stare into the fire of the eye the seeing of which is our being seen.

858. Give the All-Knowing One something to think about.

859. Elide the inexistent difference between capitalism and narco-capitalism.

860. Have fun watching everything you ever wanted to say fly out the window.

861. Gird yourself with the thread of fate.

862. Imagine how bad life would be if reality were not so terrifying.

863. Mourn everything with nothing, mourn nothing with everything.

864. Splice the film of consciousness like the video of its own beheading.

865. Feel the lightness of the universe floating nowhere, hear the darkness of the mirror.

866. Realize that you have been trying to build an airplane out of your own wings.

867. Be impressed by how I am not impressed. Impress me by not being impressed.

868. Work behind the scenes until there is no scene. Live behind the times until there is no time.

869. Pass all compliments on to your corpse.

870. Check to see if one of the wheels has fallen off—the chariot is moving in a circle.

871. Fail to buy another object in which art and theory compete to outworsen each other.

872. Be happy in the fact that nothing makes you happy.

873. Whatever is said, know that I am saying something else entirely.

874. Let the time come when there comes a time.

875. Fall in love with the apotheosis of pessimism.
876. Hear everything and still receive no word.
877. Endure everything by enduring nothing. Endure nothing by enduring everything.
878. Feel an infinite silliness suffering infinitely the absolutely unsharable knowledge of how truly serious it really is.
879. Take eternal refuge in an article.
880. Have no idea what has happened to you.
881. Become the echo within an empty tomb.
882. Perish the thinking.
883. Die so many times you forget what death is like.
884. Wake up without you: the wrong side of yourself.
885. No longer know without ever having known.
886. Find happiness, not something to make you happy.
887. Obey the infinitely unaccountable and radically immanent absence of concern.
888. Show an ounce of courage for the first time in your stupid life.
889. Look nowhere.
890. Get it way way less than you do.
891. Fashion a golden mosaic of all our glimpses.
892. Evaporate from your own view.
893. Touch the point where pain and you are the same person.

N

894. Don't ask questions when you can live in doubt.
895. Finally love the answer more than asking the question.
896. Stop wanting to think what you like to think.
897. Impose yourself on no one.
898. See that I am far more serious than I am.
899. Resurface from life as from a flooded basement.
900. Set about finding the strength necessary to enjoy me.
901. Don't worry—because worry is more worrisome than whatever it worries about. Be happy—because happiness is more happy than whatever it is happy about.
902. Fear fear way more than anything it fears.
903. Become the last thing you are interested in.
904. Stop admiring people.
905. Idolize nothing, not even that.
906. Learn to lose, lose to learn. Lose learning, learn losing.
907. Discover the real problem: that everything is actually perfect.
908. Kick yourself out of your mind.
909. Wonder if you know how much I wonder, know if you wonder how much I know.

910. Remember that the act by which you form these images is not itself an image.
911. Achieve your goal: actual experience of achieving a goal you can never achieve.
912. Face all day the massive mistake that no one wants to face.
913. Praise everything that prevents you from winning.
914. No longer want more of what you already are.
915. Crawl beyond fear and courage.
916. Fail this test.
917. Give the gift that remains when everything is given away.
918. String theory yourself along into a spiral sphere.
919. Say no to not saying yes to X no matter what.
920. Realize that you have accidentally on purpose renounced everything without realizing it.
921. Find the infinity of things inside the room with you that are neither inside nor outside the room.
922. Undermine calamity with mischievous curiosity.
923. Be not fooled by what has been rehearsing its lines for billions of years.
924. Be laughed at by the divine comedy.
925. Laugh in ON.
926. Know better.
927. Be 100% in favor of what must be done.
928. Explore the maximum intimacy of void.

929. Fight the enemy on no one's terms.

930. Forget the falseness of trying to be true, the evil of trying to be good, the ugliness of trying to be beautiful.

931. Tell me how you feel if you were real.

932. Be offended to be.

933. Adopt a zero tolerance policy on not losing.

934. Fail to catch thrownness like an auto-goal.

935. Be all you can be: the fear of losing you.

936. Stay on THAT side of the horizon.

937. Worry not whether you play the game but how you lose.

938. Since you missed your birth, at least show up for your death.

939. Place my ear to the earth and unplug the earth from my ears.

940. Notice how you lose every argument with yourself.

941. Know that reality wants to be known more than you want to know it.

942. Hunt the animal's capacity to outgrow itself.

943. Fly over the influence.

944. Die as though you were alive.

945. Hear the infinite preemptive echo of itself.

946. Please repeat THAT—all I heard was the disjunction between what you said and what you are.

947.   Fly nowhere on the wind of itself, over the seas of memory, lost being too free, in the night of the world.

948.   Jeopardize the very mode of your existence.

949.   Crack inside jokes for the outside until the laughter snaps everything back into place.

950.   Speak only in anaphorisms, prefer-not-tos that pronounce all and answer no one.

951.   Suspend movement without towards into towards without movement.

952.   Reach the summit by never getting off the ground.

953.   Win by only entering battles you have already lost.

954.   Realize just how much sense everything does not make.

955.   Become an unkillable victim of the incommunicable.

956.   Fear the impossibility of fearing anything outside yourself.

957.   Know why I want you so desperately to know what you already do.

958.   See that the demons are there because you think they are not.

959.   Scare tigers away where there aren't any.

960.   Laugh off the joke of your body.

961.   Sink higher.

962.   Find yourself on the wrong side of everything.

963. Constantly fail to not think what one cannot even think about.
964. See through the self-mirror darkly.
965. Joust in the arms of the horizon.
966. Be very afraid of belonging to any organization.
967. Cease acting like you know what to do with yourself.
968. Become an incast, lost at home in exile from nothing.
969. Spoil the party by making fun of philosophy, ruin your life with a lecture on the sigh.
970. See that however bad it is, the truth of it is not.
971. Solve the mystery of birth as direct proof of insanity.
972. Endure the evening of desire, the night of longing, the dawn of surrender.
973. Fall for the folly of photographing the infravisible.
974. Await nothing forever.
975. Stop bumping into life.
976. Prescribe Cotard syndrome to itself.
977. See each image as the picture of a tear, hearing each thought as the motion of a sigh.
978. Endure the beginning until the very end.
979. Prove yourself unreal by reading this.
980. Fail to be able to tell whether not being able to tell.
981. Follow the messenger back to the bed of the one who made you.

982.   Arrive at the unending upon the being over of what never was.
983.   Shock yourself to death by ever having thought that anything is happening.
984.   Leave yourself behind for no reason at all.
985.   Have nothing left—nothing but the nothing that is there in the beginning.
986.   Prove thyself to be nothing after all.
987.   Let occur to you what will never occur to you.
988.   Prove beyond a shadow of doubt that you are simply wrong.
989.   Focus on the only thing worth mentioning after there is absolutely nothing more to say.
990.   Internally avoid pronouns like the plague.
991.   Be blinded by what a tear sees.
992.   Exit the strategy.
993.   Die by remaining cheerful.
994.   Be killed to life by a dream.
995.   Notice that the whole thing is impossible from the start.
996.   Be as different as life itself.
997.   See the eye as the blindspot of itself and the other.
998.   Listen to music without the sound.
999.   Ask what it means never to ask what it means.
1000.   Settle that it is not settled.
1001.   Wake from the dream of being awake.

1002.   Stop it from happening to you by no longer saying 'me'.
1003.   Turn things out to not.
1004.   Do not make much of things.
1005.   Observe the image where it is more real.
1006.   No longer refuse to see what the whole universe actually is.
1007.   Unposition the future.
1008.   Land at the point where sophisticated historically-contextualized self-consciousness is as irrelevant as it has always been.
1009.   Be dwarfed to zero by all that you have intimated.
1010.   Be here not.
1011.   Plan only the this—the moment of realization that you are as stupid as everyone else.
1012.   Fight at the front line of every war: you.
1013.   HJave nothing to do with religion or politics.
1014.   Surround yourself with no one.
1015.   Give the nothingness of yourself to everyone you see.
1016.   Make sure no one has seen you recently.
1017.   Be here, be destroyed.
1018.   Sleep through the veil between birth and death.
1019.   Perform a lifetime.
1020.   Hear always a name whose sound makes breath a blinking of the heart's eye.
1021.   No longer know how to live.
1022.   Give thanks for never having been.

1023. Run automatically at the speed at which the heart-lamp burns a hole through the film of consciousness.

1024. Apologize for having ever thought anything.

1025. Follow one thing to another to itself.

1026. Dwell in a fantasy world of your own decreation.

1027. Become one great ear.

1028. Punish WE until it is unable to speak without special permission.

1029. Eliminate WE to the max.

1030. Drink the bliss that makes your eyes set moths on fire.

1031. Terrify the enemy with the sight of your own severed head.

1032. Sell yourself into slavery.

1033. Spend everything on what cannot be bought.

1034. Avoid presenting the paper before you have suffered its truth.

1035. Walk tall in prostrate gratitude that you never were.

1036. Swing gently in the noose of inescaping sighs.

1037. Drown all day long in the scream of ...

1038. Try not to nurture anyone.

1039. Accelerate sound past the future of light speed.

1040. Never stop waking up by always failing to distinguish between dream and waking.

1041. Enter the cave of escape. Exit the hatch of exit.
1042. Find the point at which your veins start sucking the vampire into your blood through its own teeth.
1043. Link to itself.
1044. Sleep below the floor and wake up above the ceiling.
1045. Snag your tooth on space and trip your eye on time.
1046. Aatch a dream wake up without you.
1047. Crawl under the situation in which it is possible you actually exist.
1048. Scar the void.
1049. Be exiled from the country of you.
1050. Non-improve reality.
1051. See where I is.
1052. Perform zero for the sake of nothing.
1053. Desire, long, surrender, die, repeat …
1054. Be the one who walks you corpse to the grave.
1055. Find consolation in the madness-option.
1056. Loose the arrow of the sigh that no one sighs.
1057. Ask not what to do with this.
1058. Have no reason to be pessimistic or optimistic.
1059. Neutralize the end.
1060. Write a book that speaks like your severed head.
1061. Become a ghoast.
1062. Consider only three authorship options: forged, pseudonymous, posthumous.

1063. Say yes to the no in the now.
1064. Establish facts smarter than ideas.
1065. Make a cut between the beginning of the middle of the end and the end of the beginning of the middle.
1066. Consider to whom your blood belongs.
1067. Block yourself.
1068. Firmly establish thyself within an order of existential confusion from which the world, the flesh, and the devil forever flee in terror.
1069. Join the planet-wide campaign to replace all sad, angry, and worried looks with buttons that read "Defeated by Life."
1070. Hasten to where meaning becomes too meaningless and meaninglessness too meaningful.
1071. Imagine not that what never existed in the first place can become extinct.
1072. Don't not confuse yourself with the sorrow you feel for yourself.
1073. Attend another talk on what talking should do, inside a panel on the possibilities of the panel, towards a conference on the future of conferences.
1074. Prepare to lose, whether you fight God or not.
1075. Update the status of yourself to never mind.
1076. Be the dream that makes me forget the whole dream.

1077. Lose all one's marbles and see them floating in the heavens as far as the eye can see.
1078. Only backbite everyone all at once.
1079. Play peak-a-byss in paradise with baby universes.
1080. Race with the light that flees the lightning.
1081. Be pronounced by the Astonishing Inner Underworld of Overwhelming Experience.
1082. Lasciami in rapace.
1083. Be not wise.
1084. Allow omniscience to write that letter for you.
1085. Run into the ground of thy beseeching.
1086. Figure out that having grown up and being here are mutually exclusive.
1087. Bump into the someone who is taking yourself for a walk.
1088. Walk out in the middle of the universal movie.
1089. Feel inexplicably and subtly weird all over, like something from beyond the shoreless shore is about to pounce in your pulse.
1090. Blacken beautifully thy human face with an uncontrollable surplus of boisterous sobbing.
1091. Meet me in the Hyperborean cathedral of frozen tears.
1092. Calmly shout a silent hyperfriendly soul-scream across all distance.

1093.   Lose your voice by Julian of Norwich feeding to Margery Kempe the ball that Clarice Lispector rolled out of your throat-lump.

1094.   Accept ( )holeheartedly everything and nothing.

1095.   Feel pretty sure the problem has something to do with wanting anything at all.

1096.   Let everything else have something to say, not you.

1097.   Don't say nothing, be everything.

1098.   No longer care about anything and go on loving no one for no reason eternally.

1099.   Be without recourse to being, without recourse to recourse, and without without.

1100.   Avoid the mistake of thinking you know how to live.

1101.   Calmly sketch the mountainous waves of inner storm.

1102.   See the whole universe blinding itself in a paroxysm of sorrow.

1103.   Win by losing and lose by winning the competition between a loss that wins and a win that loses.

1104.   Explain not.

1105.   Don't let the universe rub off on you.

1106.   Swim the net to freedom.

1107.   Use language from a hyper-losing position of total chesslessness.

1108.   Say everything without saying.

1109.   Sink so far that the summit becomes a mountain climber in search of you.

1110.   Stop lying by thinking the world is there.

1111.   Know not how to say this solely on the basis of not knowing whether saying is possible.

1112.   Discover that you are the kind of fish that mistakes the hook for the bait.

1113.   Make it to the point where point itself gets up and walks away.

1114.   Pursue the peril of letting one's throat-lump speak for oneself on the last day of everything.

1115.   Think from the point where every single thought begins with 'you have no idea'.

1116.   Steer clear of yourself on the ocean of …

1117.   Sign a universal, infinitely binding pact to never again think, feel, or act about yourself.

1118.   Lifesave the heart that goes swimming in the heart.

1119.   Harmlessly ruin yourself forever through no fault of your own.

1120.   Lose the mind you never had.

1121.   Find rest in the fact that life simply consists of continual weeping.

1122.   Hunt yourself empty-handed in the forest of restless sorrow and come back trussed up on a raft down the river of no return.

1123.   Lose the battle between wanting and wanting to want nothing.

1124.   Stop pretending to not see that I am dying a thousand times a day.

1125.   Still no longer fathom the depth of what did not happen.

1126.   Enjoy the eternal honor of being the not-yourself who stole no one's heart.

1127.   Double a zero through itself into the menagerie of infinity.

1128.   Scare away all the scared people by running toward the Monster.

1129.   Chase yourself out of the woods of longing and despair.

1130.   Drive the spear in further by walking in any direction.

1131.   Let everything explain itself perfectly.

1132.   Succeed at near success suddenly followed by total failure.

1133.   Stop being impressed by the demonstration of skill—there is nothing to it.

1134.   Live in the tomb of love undying.

1135.   Ecstatically confess a high degree of idiocy.

1136.   Out the closet.

1137.   Hear that the snake sounds like a rope.

1138.   Show up where no longer being is the only way of seeing anything every again.

1139.   Hear love never divulge its reason for loving.

1140.   Hear reason never divulge its love of reasoning.

1141.   See that you are nothing next to the forces at work within you.

1142.   Be still and know that I am gone.
1143.   Listen to what I say after you filter out the whirring in my mind.
1144.   Confirm that life has vanished.
1145.   Be yourself, the worst that can happen to you.
1146.   Ovulate with one's eyes.
1147.   Hyperopically dilate the pupilverse into swallowing the cosmic egg.
1148.   Blind the horizon with a wink.
1149.   Sink into terminal suspicion that there is neither inside nor outside, only an all-significant simplicity impossible to fathom.
1150.   Feed the disease with thoughts of cure.
1151.   Lose wit, let syllables fall, so that the unsaid, may express all.
1152.   Be guilty of being you.
1153.   Drown in the incommensurable.
1154.   Become eternal by waiting for (an) eternity.
1155.   Stay in the conversation by shouting silence.
1156.   Formulate the reason they only want truth in argument form.
1157.   Come to the truth of this by the same way that anything is happening at all.
1158.   Let presumptuous eagerness be disappointed.
1159.   Fall to the ground upon which this your inexistence hangs.
1160.   Experience life-threatening difficulty understanding why people are saying

what they are saying the way they are saying it and why.

1161. Be pierced with the kind of arrow whose removal turns the whole universe inside out.

1162. Instruct yourself to fail.

1163. Effortlessly amass further proof that this world is not your home.

1164. Admit it.

1165. Be fatally wounded with forever.

1166. Impale thyself on an infinite spear of distilled crystal tears.

1167. Trash the universe before it is too late.

1168. Cure me of the dream of you.

1169. Be happy in sorrow, mourn in joy.

1170. Pretend not to have infected my soul.

1171. Hear my deafness speak—irrationally—to your muteness.

1172. Infinitely accept the gift of giving yourself up.

1173. See everything so amazing that there is nothing quite like it.

1174. Melt the mountain, swallow the sky, drown the ocean, become all tear.

1175. Consider what to do if you can't stand to be a subject of experience anymore.

1176. Fade out of the world into and from which you were never born.

1177. Tell a Cotardian delusionist to get a life.

1178. Try not to act as if life were not a fatal wound.

1179. Stop pretending you are the first person to suffer being you.

1180.   See it everywhere, find it in nothing.
1181.   Desire our zero, belong to this trust,
        resign everything, and love all to dust.
1182.   Run out of time.
1183.   Don't mistake mercury for crystal or
        liquid crystal for either.
1184.   Never again be tricked by threat of
        losing what you never had to begin with.
1185.   Feast on not devouring the idolized fear
        you are feeding off of.
1186.   Destroy the enemy with no one to defeat
        it.
1187.   Be relegated to the no-one category.
1188.   Define time as the speed at which you
        notice that nothing ever happens and
        space as the place where you see that
        everything already has.
1189.   Imagine the intelligence it takes to make
        nothing work out.
1190.   Seek out that which gets under the skin
        of everything.
1191.   Think the world if it stopped worrying.
1192.   Bask in beauty until your decapitation is
        beheaded.
1193.   Read it like Cioran without the jokes.
1194.   Wonder whether there is a price for
        remembering something forever.
1195.   Lose the battle between the absolute
        maximization of insignificance and the
        infinite intensification of meaning.
1196.   Feel free to feel indescribably strange
        about everything.

1197. Take antipodal paths to meet on this side of the other earth.

1198. Still have a shot at being wrong one's entire life.

1199. Pit the power of all reasons against the impotence of all explanations.

1200. Lose yourself in the debate between what head says about heart and what heart says about head.

1201. Search every corner of your heart until your heart is everywhere.

1202. Return here after seeing absolutely everything.

1203. Stand on the edge of the cliff where no new experience will do it for you.

1204. Become a body moved by a breath, a breath moved by a thought, a thought moved by a body.

1205. Portray the impression between every two things.

1206. Inhale you the more I exhale me—inhale me the more I exhale you.

1207. Ob-alliterate thyself beyond being.

1208. Win the philosophical race between horse, horsiness, and horseness.

1209. Know not where the word comes from, who hears it, or where it goes.

1210. Leap lightly into darkness.

1211. See fog as sunshine.

1212. Stop dreaming this universe, wake up from yourself, and take a look around.

1213. Tug on the chain of being until all hearts skip a beat.

1214.   Unlive life as neither end, beginning, nor middle.

1215.   Swim safe as a tardigrade through the hydrothermal vents of your deepest soul-wound.

1216.   Practice individuation by birth, death by individuation, and life by death.

1217.   Admit that birth is not the first time you failed to solve that problem.

1218.   Lay my head on the pillow of your pupils—a guillotine of dreams.

1219.   Lock me in a room without myself.

1220.   Answer messages by not existing.

1221.   No longer be there for yourself.

1222.   Don't happen.

1223.   Become the only excuse for being.

1224.   Accept responsibility for being how it all came to this.

1225.   Weep away the dream.

1226.   Be fatally wounded with forever.

1227.   Fall more and more in love with reality seeing how much less and less sense it makes.

1228.   Take credit for being the beginning of my end.

1229.   Suddenly see that this is.

1230.   Reconsider every hour the level at which you actually live.

1231.   Stay forever with never: Never born, never die. Never cured, never sick. Never found, never lost. Never with, never without. Never arrived, never departed.

1232.   Never have been at home.
1233.   Trim the burning fringes of being.
1234.   Abandon all hope, ye who exit.
1235.   Be the worst that can happen to you.
1236.   Answer 'what's wrong with me?' with you.
1237.   Terminally suspect that there is neither inside nor outside, only an all-significant simplicity impossible to fathom.
1238.   Live all day in the dumbest of questions.
1239.   Play tag with no one.
1240.   Discover your true self: the only problem in existence.
1241.   Realize that this universe is the insane asylum you should have checked yourself into aeons ago.
1242.   Find the one you will only ever see again by never having been.
1243.   Don't have the faintest idea what you are talking about and still mean everything you say.
1244.   Faint by hearing what I do not say.
1245.   Take all my strength to not use any of it.
1246.   Find a totally new way to renounce everything.
1247.   Take me away from myself forever.
1248.   Find the summit from the bottom of the sea.
1249.   Return to where no one ever was, neither you nor me.
1250.   Don't get the point—let it get you.

1251.   Perceive your own nothingness as the pupil of reality.

1252.   Abandon bipedalism for worm-swimming with the soul's own slowness.

1253.   Dizzily feel everything is so much that it is hard to see how anyone stands anything at all.

1254.   Crave no power other than the ability to say someone's name.

1255.   Unfriend everyone who cares what happens.

1256.   Stay for the Acceleration.

1257.   Forget dying with living and know life with the dead.

1258.   Understand that no one will take it personally if you do not care about anything anymore.

1259.   Help yourself be tied to the stake.

1260.   Mis-aim another massively wayward prayer-cannon fired by no one into nowhere.

1261.   Realize God by embarrassing yourself beyond belief.

1262.   Make a note to yourself: "Thanks for your message. I am away now and will get back to you as soon as I can't."

1263.   Communicate with yourself on auto-reply.

1264.   Don't think this is the first time someone is born and lives and dies in a single state of total confusion.

1265.   See that I am not here either.

1266. Know that no one has ever understood a single thought.

1267. Realize that each of your thoughts has already been thought by a trillion hyper-intelligent entities none of whom gets it.

1268. Simply don't trust life to take you where you need to go.

1269. Fall victim to an infinitely incompatible aesthetics.

1270. Secretly say so much to no one that you forget how to breathe.

1271. Overreact to being.

1272. Realize that no one has ever understood a thing you said nor ever will.

1273. Suspect that you are not the most important thing in the universe after all.

1274. Never sign your name to yourself.

1275. Look everywhere except here.

1276. Experiment with the absence of you.

1277. Meet yourself where the failure of mysticism meets the mysticism of failure.

1278. Flop into place.

1279. Decide not to write a book entitled *As As As*.

1280. Never fail to blow your finest moment.

1281. Know one thing that makes nothing else matter.

1282. Stay in the pit until the pit is in thee.

1283. Owe it to yourself to know that no one owes you anything.

1284. Fail from all perspectives except none.

1285.   Contract a disease made worse by every cure.
1286.   Find refuge in the identity of what makes you want to die and the only thing worth living for.
1287.   Choose between losing one's mind and never having one in the first place.
1288.   Stop liking things that are about you.
1289.   Shrink the strange loop to zero in a tangle of silence.
1290.   Collapse!
1291.   Fail to lose the fight to avoid young Werther's fate.
1292.   Entomb every tomb in its own floating sink whole.
1293.   Learn to postpone the immediacy of everything.
1294.   Choke on the riddle of oneself until you smile.
1295.   Be mistaken for a poet when saying what you know and for a philosopher when saying what you feel.
1296.   Just think: matter is immaterial, energy is weak, mind is stupid, and soul is whatever—so there!
1297.   Bite upward with a cosmic egg tooth, shaped like the silence of the outside.
1298.   Feed me my hunger until I vomit forth all that was, is, and will be.
1299.   Speak the same language as no one.
1300.   Feel how utterly beyond—within—everything one really is.

1301. Flop out of the fish tank of artificial happiness.
1302. See that there is only one problem and it is not a problem.
1303. Wrap the knot of you around the spiral of truth.
1304. Swim against the mechanical mind-flow.
1305. See how the devil cannot see himself.
1306. Hear the voice where dreamer, dreamed, and dream are one say nothing.
1307. Rest in the reality of absolute disorientation—everything in place.
1308. Trade it all in one of these days.
1309. Comprehend that that the universe is is bigger than the universe and that it never was is bigger than both.
1310. Don't worry, there is no reason to be here.
1311. Show me how to avoid myself.
1312. Expect no straight answer from the crooked.
1313. Use all your strength to do nothing.
1314. Make a point of waking before the dream dies.
1315. Take it easy—this is all just reality playing a trick on itself.
1316. Paint yourself with a colour out of space.
1317. Take time as the time it takes to wake up.
1318. Catch yourself red-handed without any hands and find yourself in the middle of not finding anything.

1319.   Float above space on a mountain and
        drift beyond time in a cloud.
1320.   Discover yourself as living proof that
        you are not alive
1321.   Lose all the races between winning and
        losing, wining and winning, and losing
        and losing.
1322.   Multiply and divide what is said by the
        fact that it is said.
1323.   Never stop noticing who talks about
        who.
1324.   Ask yourself a questioner.
1325.   Realize that you died of boredom ages
        ago and this is your afterlife.
1326.   Experience the indifference.
1327.   Wake from this dream by remembering
        how you died.
1328.   Be ready to perish at any moment.
1329.   Experience the infinite relief of realizing
        that one is a total idiot.
1330.   Realize that nothing whatsoever makes
        sense, starting with all that you love.
1331.   Say hello to the worm whose casting
        your body will be.
1332.   Ascend the mountain one atom at a
        time.
1333.   Gladden thyself in the sunny air of pure
        despair.
1334.   See so many connections that there is
        nothing to see.
1335.   Draw so many distinctions that you go
        blind.

1336. Take dictation how to be happy from the nightmare of yourself.

1337. Pre-empt the inevitable, post-empt the always already.

1338. Write with a dagger in the heart of void.

1339. Live the dream without the dream.

1340. Only bother with the weight that requires 100% of your non-strength to lift.

1341. Grasp your enormous error up to now.

1342. Be silent to the human symphony of phony sympathy.

1343. Locate the answer in the form of a bullet in the head of the questioner.

1344. Fail hagiography.

1345. Stop presenting yourself as a person.

1346. Take all the pieces out one garbage at a time.

1347. Behead me with the key to your heart.

1348. Weep for no reason at the sight of yourself.

1349. Drown the ocean.

1350. Dwell in the jungle where the jungle disappears.

1351. Fade time.

1352. Don't be at fault—more like fault itself.

1353. Swallow yourself without know the way out.

1354. Drink the ocean, not a drop of it yours.

1355. Live in a world in which if you talk about the world you die.

1356. Die in a world in which if you don't talk about the world you never were.

1357.   Collaborate with no one.

1358.   Gaze heavenward until your pupils are impaled by a falling sigh.

1359.   See how far my heart sank when I saw anything.

1360.   Love what never ends with a never-ending love.

1361.   Cut out your tongue with the edge of a dream.

gnOme is a secret press specializing in the publication of anonymous, pseudepigraphical, and apocryphal works from the past, present, and future.

"Be no one!" (Anonymous).

gnOme is acephalic. Book sales support the authors.

GNOMEBOOKS.WORDPRESS.COM

Other titles from gnOme

A & N • *Autophagiography*

Brian O'Blivion • *Blackest Ever Hole*

Cergat • *Earthmare: The Lost Book of Wars*

Eva Clanculator • *Atheologica Germanica*

Ars Cogitanda • *footnote to* silence

M.O.N. • *ObliviOnanisM*

Pseudo-Leopardi • *Cantos for the Crestfallen*

I. P. Snooks *Be Still, My Throbbing Tattoo*

Rasu-Yong Tugen, Baroness De Tristeombre •
Songs from the Black Moon

Subject A • *Verses from the Underlands*

Y.O.U. • *How to Stay in Hell*

M • *Un-Sight/ Un-Sound (delirium X.)*

HWORDE

Nab Saheb and Denys X. Arbaris • *Bergmetal:
Oro-Emblems of the Musical Beyond*

Yuu Seki • *Serial Kitsch*